healing with yoga

a holistic way to unite body and mind

for greater wellbeing and serenity

Doriel Hall

HERMES HOUSE

The edition published by Hermes House

Hermes House is an imprint of Anness Publishing Limited,
Hermes House, 88–89 Blackfriars Road, London SE1 8HA

Publisher: Joanna Lorenz
Production Controller: Joanna King

Publisher's Note:

The Reader should not regard the recommendations, ideas and techniques expressed and described in this book as substitutes for the advice of a qualified medical practitioner or other qualified professional. Any use to which the recommendations, ideas and techniques are put is at the reader's sole discretion and risk.

Printed in Hong Kong/China

3 5 7 9 10 8 6 4

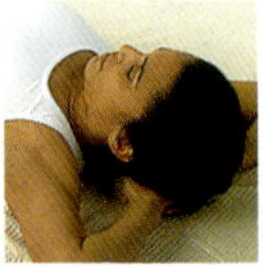

contents

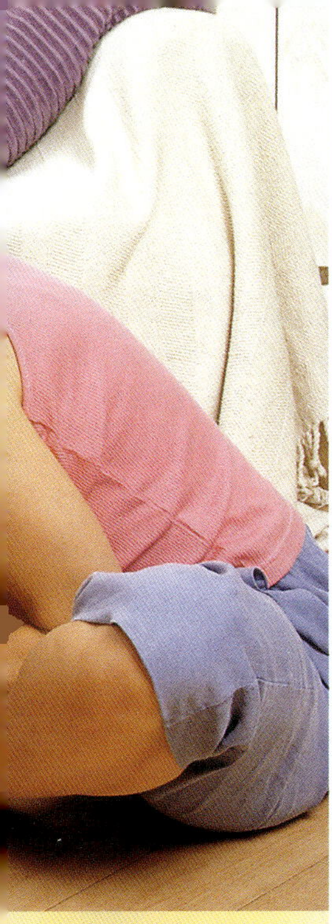

introduction

Yoga has been practised for thousands of years to bring stillness to the mind and health and vitality to the body. Today, we are rediscovering how this ancient art can be used to bring healing into our lives, especially by rebalancing the nervous system, which is thrown out of balance by the stressful demands of modern life. In the Sanskrit language, the word "yoga" means union, harmony and balance. This is what regular yoga practice achieves, both within ourselves and in our relationship with the world around us, through techniques that include postures (*asanas*), breathing (*pranayama*), meditation and resolve (*sankalpa*).

Healing and self-healing

We all need healing, which simply means changing for the better at one or more levels of our being – the physical, energetic, nervous, thinking and attitudinal aspects. These five levels, called the koshas in yoga, are interactive.

The koshas

These levels can be pictured as invisible layers, emanating outwards from the solid physical body (the first level). We feel the energy body as we approach someone or when they invade our space. The nervous system picks up signals from outside via our five senses. Our thoughts travel across space and even time. Our attitudes shape our destinies through eternity.

When we meditate we can become aware that these five levels of our being also flow inwards, contacting the vibrations of the spirit. These levels make up "who we are".

Successful healing brings us – the whole person – into our optimum state of harmony and wellbeing by treating not only our physical symptoms but also any energy disruptions, nervous imbalances, mental overload or deep

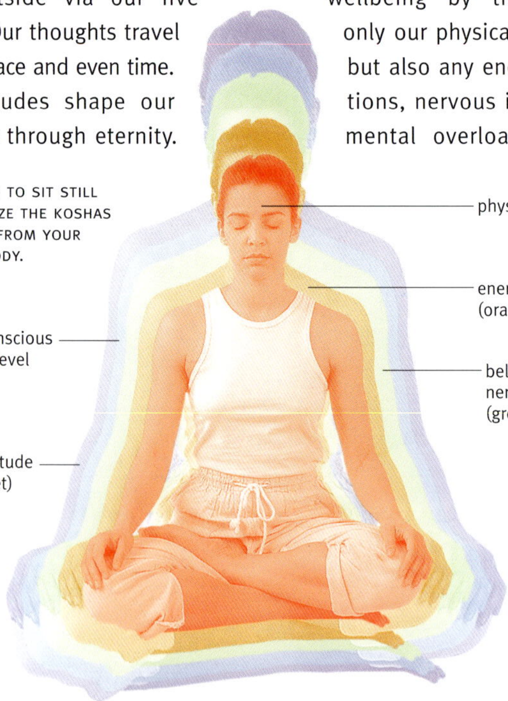

▸ Take time to sit still and visualize the koshas emanating from your physical body.

▲ Practising yoga with your children creates a great sense of togetherness.

"soul sickness" that may be affecting us. This alters our whole outlook on life, even allowing us to live peacefully with symptoms or circumstances that previously caused us great distress.

Self-healing with yoga

In yoga we take responsibility for our own wellbeing through the practice of self-discipline, self-awareness and self-surrender. Self-discipline simply means "sticking at it", practising yoga regularly, with enthusiasm and commitment. A few breaths and stretches here and there during quiet moments, plus a regular daily session of half-an-hour or so, is ideal – but any yoga is better than none at all and will still bring great results over time. Joining a weekly yoga class is a good idea and can inspire us to develop our practice further.

Self-awareness is essential for safety in practice. If anything feels wrong, stop doing it. Yoga is non-competitive, so we learn to know and accept how we feel today and to practise accordingly. Yoga is a state of relaxed alertness at all times. Self-surrender means letting go of our comfortable habits and familiar mindsets to make room for healthier ones. Our body lets go of its worn-out cells as new ones are formed. In the same way, we must let go of our worn-out opinions, prejudices, habits, self-image and other burdens.

The nervous system

The nervous system is related to the middle kosha that links the physical and energetic levels (or "body" koshas), with the thinking and attitudinal levels (or "mind" koshas). The system has several branches; yoga works on them all.

The middle kosha contains all the unconscious aspects of the mind, such as the memory, instinct, and programmed responses, as well as the nervous system that allows the conscious mind to communicate with the body and to turn thoughts into physical actions. The brain and spinal cord provide the main "motorway" for nervous impulses to travel along the nerve cells to and from all parts of the body. It is vital to keep this "traffic" flowing freely.

▼ YOGA TEACHES US THAT WE CAN CONSCIOUSLY CHOOSE WHEN TO RELAX.

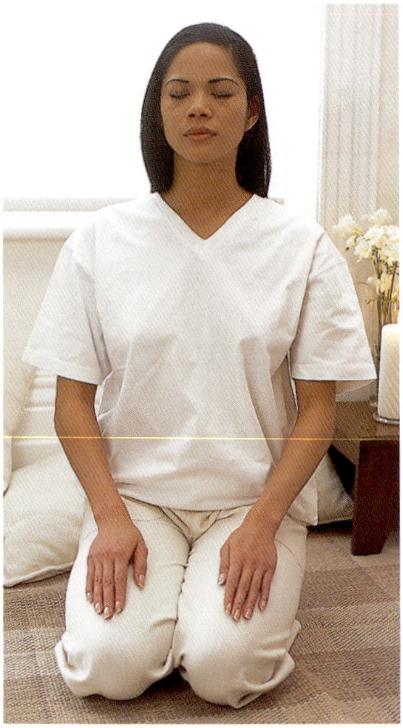

Yoga makes us more aware through the sensory nervous system: our sight, hearing, touch, taste and smell become more alert and responsive. It makes us more skilful in movement through the motor nervous system, which tells each muscle when to contract and by how much. It even allows us to access the autonomic nervous system, so that we can choose consciously when to be keyed up or relaxed while maintaining our inner serenity.

THE AUTONOMIC NERVOUS SYSTEM

This system maintains homeostasis (internal harmony) by controlling the respiratory, cardiovascular, digestive, hormonal, immune and other involuntary body systems.

Its two complementary branches work together like the accelerator and brakes in a car. One branch "revs up" certain systems to help us deal with imminent physical danger. This is known as the "fright-fight-flight" response and it is needed for surviving external threats. The other branch deals with nourishment, long-term maintenance, rest and repair. It is responsible for ensuring our longer-term health and survival. Most of us fail to appreciate that we do not have the resources to attend to both these aspects at the same time. If we spend too much time in fight-or-flight mode, we are neglecting to digest our food or repair our damaged cells, and tiredness and poor health will inevitably follow.

Our nervous systems have not yet evolved to cope with the profound changes in lifestyle wrought by our technological society, which is only about 200 years old. Today, our lives are highly stressful, competitive and go-getting, making us feel angry, frustrated, confused and anxious a lot of the time, and it is not surprising that many of us get stuck in the fright-fight-flight syndrome. Since there is no physical enemy for us to kill or escape from, the stress hormones in our bodies remain unused. These can build up to dangerous levels and eventually lead to serious diseases. Our nervous systems may become totally out of balance, with the accelerator on full throttle nearly all the time.

▲ Keep your spine loose and supple to help your nervous system do its work.

The autonomic nervous system may seem to be beyond our conscious control, but fortunately we can influence it through yoga, helping us to regain internal harmony and balance.

The spine's energy motorway

The spine houses a subtle "motorway" that carries the life force in our energy body. As it enters or leaves at the "roundabouts" or chakras, this life force is a blend of all our energies: physical, vital, nervous, mental and attitudinal.

If the spine's energy "motorway" is obstructed the "side roads" become blocked and their territory is deprived of essential nourishment, communications, and the ability to remove toxic wastes. The resulting distress is called "illness". You can keep the traffic flowing smoothly in the spine through the use of posture, movements with breath awareness, visualization, relaxation and meditation.

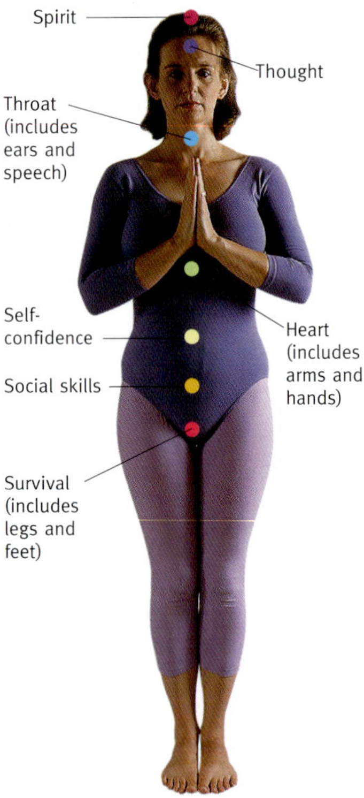

◂ The chakras represent the three energies of Life, Light and Love.

The chakras

Energy enters and leaves our spine through the chakras. These are also associated with the three important cavities in our bodies. The abdominal cavity protects our vital organs and houses three major chakras dealing with the energies of Life: survival, social interaction and self-confidence. The legs and feet are extensions of our survival chakra. Great emphasis is placed in yoga upon strengthening the lower body so that we can cope with the challenges of living.

The skull cavity lies at the top of the spine and protects the brain. It houses two major chakras concerned with the energies of

▲ *Savasana* is a classic example of spinal alignment.

awareness and wisdom or Light. Breathing and balancing exercises switch on the Light in our heads, giving us greater understanding in both yoga and daily life.

Lying between the skull and abdominal cavities is the thoracic cavity. This protects our hearts and lungs and houses the two chakras concerned with relationship or Love energies. The arms and hands are extensions of the heart chakra (for reaching out to others) and the ears and mouth are extensions of the throat chakra (for communicating). Simply thinking about someone engages relationship (Love) energies, even if we don't actually like them. Yoga gradually increases our capacity for unconditional love and cancels out negative thoughts and feelings. Backbends and chest expanding exercises help to open and lift the upper body, allowing Love energy to flow more freely. It also improves our breathing and circulation.

▶ In *Tadasana*, you are aligning your spine while fighting the forces of gravity. It is a simple yet strong pose.

Breathing patterns

Yoga helps us to change our breathing. Slow, deep breathing through the nose relaxes the heart and sends "all is well" messages to the brain. Once we have learned yoga breathing habits we can lessen our stress and anxiety.

A fast, shallow breathing pattern, with panting or gasping through the mouth to "snatch" more air, is usually the result of stress. This type of breathing strains the heart and makes the stress worse. It also sends panic messages to the brain, which then revs up the fright-fight-flight response and a vicious circle is created: "Quick! Fight harder! Run away faster!" Since we cannot physically fight the boss nor flee from a traffic jam, we end up feeling even more anxious and stressed.

The diaphragm is the chief "breathing muscle". It lies across the base of the chest, separating it from the abdomen above the waist (and stomach). When we breathe in, it flattens downwards, massaging the abdominal organs. When we breathe out it relaxes upwards into the chest. "Deep" yoga breathing is diaphragmatic breathing. In yoga postures the breath is co-ordinated with both stretching and moving energy.

KNEELING POSE, *VAJRASANA*

▲ Sit on your heels, with big toes touching underneath you. Tuck your tailbone under and tilt your pelvis backwards, to avoid hollowing your lumbar spine. Clasp your hands in your lap and stretch the spine up, lifting and opening your chest. Keep your chin and shoulders down. Breathe slowly and deeply a few times in this position and focus on feeling the breathing movements within.

Arm and chest stretch with breath

▲ Sit in *vajrasana* (see opposite). Now, as you breathe IN, kneel up and stretch your clasped hands directly overhead, with your palms up. Breathe OUT and stretch up even more. Breathe IN to sit on heels and OUT to lower hands to lap. Repeat the sequence a few times, co-ordinating breath and movements. The arm stretch, with the breath, can also be done when standing or sitting on a chair.

Body-mind breathing cycle

Now add the feeling of moving energy up and down the spine, which calms, balances and heals the nervous system. The general rule is to move energy upwards through the spine on the breath IN and to stretch and energize the limbs on the breath OUT. You may need several breaths to perfect a posture. End by breathing OUT to bring energy down and relax.

▲ Put palms together with your elbows out to the side. Stand in a comfortable upright position. Pull the spine up and breathe IN, squeezing the inner thighs and pelvic floor muscles. Breathe OUT, squeezing corset muscles at waist. Breathe IN, pressing palms together and squeezing spinal muscles behind the heart to lift and open the chest. Breathe OUT to relax. Repeat three times.

Spinal alignment

Good spinal posture is vital to the health and wellbeing of all five koshas. It allows free passage of nervous impulses between the body cells and the brain, and of vital energy within and between the chakras.

Dangers of poor posture

Many common health problems are linked to poor posture. Besides causing compression in certain nerve pathways and disharmony in the chakras, poor posture also causes physical problems around the areas where the spine is out of alignment. Blockages in the structural, nervous or energy systems will reveal themselves in time through congestion, distress, pain and eventually disease around the area involved.

Common problems

Rigidity in the pelvic and sacral area puts pressure on the hip, knee, ankle and foot joints, and the ligaments. This pressure eventually makes movement, and walking, difficult and painful.

▼ Do you recognize any of these common postural problems in yourself?

Compression of the digestive organs results in insufficient oxygenated blood causing them to malfunction. This can lead to infection as the stale blood is not removed.

▲ WHEN STANDING CORRECTLY, THE BODY IS BALANCED AND THE SPINE STRETCHED UP.

Compression of the cervical spine (causing a jutting chin) is a frequent cause of headaches and mouth breathing, which can itself cause nasal and sinus congestion.

A weakness in the thoracic spine (which causes a concave chest) can result in the compression of the diaphragm and intercostal muscles. This can lead to poor breathing, chest infections, lung congestion and heart and circulation problems.

Compression in the lumbar spine (caused largely by weak abdominal muscles) results in all kinds of lower back and leg pain (including trapped nerves and sciatica) and failure to hold the lower organs in place. This can lead to problems such as prolapse and incontinence.

Some problems are caused by structural abnormalities, and yoga can often help. Most of the above problems, however, are due to poor posture, which is apt to deteriorate further with age or excessive weight gain. Fortunately, they can be halted and even reversed through gentle and persistent yoga practice, especially those practices that improve spinal alignment through movement and isometric "muscle squeezing" done standing, kneeling, sitting or lying.

The chakras, or vitality centres, can also be energized and balanced when breathing and visualization practices are combined with an awareness of spinal alignment. A strong lower body allows the upper body to lift and open.

Improving posture

This isometric "muscle-squeezing" exercise will improve your posture. Do it lying on your back, sitting, kneeling or standing. Practise it anywhere and often, to replace poor postural habits with good ones.

ISOMETRIC EXERCISE

1 Stretch up through your spine. Press the palms together at heart level before lifting your elbows to shoulder height.

2 Begin by tightening the muscles of the inner thighs (at the top near the groin). Involve the backs of the thighs as well, but keep the buttocks relaxed. Squeeze an actual or imaginary jar between the thighs. These muscles help to support the trunk when standing.

3 Next tighten the pelvic floor muscles. These muscles also help to support the weight of the trunk. Squeeze as though pulling the base of the body up inside. Weakness in the pelvic floor muscles causes lower back pain, sexual problems and also incontinence (especially after childbirth).

▾ ISOMETRIC EXERCISE INVOLVES ALMOST IMPERCEPTIBLE BUT POWERFUL MOVEMENTS.

4 Now tilt the pelvis slightly by tucking the tailbone under. Lift the pubic bone by tightening the lower abdominal and groin muscles. These muscles help to hold the sacral spine in alignment, correcting excess lumbar curvature and pressure on the sacroiliac joints.

5 Tighten the corset muscles (the transverse abdominals), pulling the waist and navel back towards the spine. This holds the lumbar spine in place and prevents abdominal sagging. Your energy will sweep spontaneously up through your chest, neck, head and crown, as you realign them by opening the chest, lifting the ears away from the shoulders and bringing the head in line with the spine.

6 The sacrospinalis muscles on each side of the thoracic spine hold it upright and keep the chest open. Pressing the palms hard together activates these muscles and lifts the chest. Breathe IN strongly, drawing your energy down from the crown, bringing Light into your body and mind, and opening yourself to the Love energies radiating from your "divine core".

▲ Tightening the corset muscles keeps the torso erect and energy flowing.

Watchpoint

Do not squeeze the pelvic floor or abdominal muscles if you are pregnant, after recent abdominal surgery or have serious digestive problems. Instead, focus on lifting up through the lower, middle and upper spine.

7 To release this posture, breathe OUT slowly and deeply. Take your energy down to your feet then relax, releasing all physical, mental and emotional "waste products". Let them become neutralized by the Earth. Do three rounds only. Repeat this exercise frequently.

Letting go

Deep relaxation is an essential part of yoga practice, whether it is a short rest between exercises or fifteen blissful minutes ending with your resolve, or *sankalpa*. The shoulders and hips hold tension and should be eased first.

Making a resolve

We feel happy and at peace when we relax. We can retain this feeling afterwards by changing some of our unhelpful attitudes towards life while we are in the relaxed state. If life is a journey we can choose either to "climb mountains" (difficulty and struggle) or to "go with the flow" (relaxing and letting go). It is up to us, but making room for change means letting go of negative or outdated beliefs and trusting the Cosmos (or God, the Universal Life Force or Spirit) to guide us into the future.

Sankalpa

Meaning "resolve", *sankalpa* is a yoga practice for changing our attitudes. We can change the energies in any of our chakras, building up more vitality (Life), awareness (Light) or positive attitudes in our relationships (Love) by practising *sankalpa* in deep relaxation.

Before entering into relaxation, we choose how we want to be and form a statement in simple words, starting with phrases such as "From this moment on I am becoming more and more ..." or "I am feeling more and more ..." or simply "I am ...". Use only positive words that make you feel good about yourself. Be positive. Avoid words that suggest the possibility of failure, such as "try", or words that reinforce your present condition, such as "less tired/negative/depressed" and so on. Avoid projecting into the future with statements saying "I will be/feel/ become ...", remembering that change can only happen in the here and now.

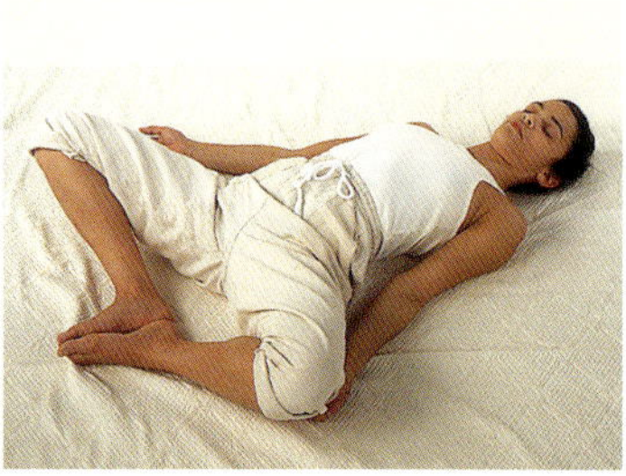

▲ The butterfly stretch is a relaxing pose for deep breathing and loosening the hip joints.

Choose only one quality at a time for your *sankalpa*, and stick with it until it is no longer needed. Repeat the same *sankalpa* every time you relax, also upon waking and before going to sleep. Meanwhile live your life as if you already have the quality you are developing. When your *sankalpa* is established, make a new one.

Savasana, corpse pose

This is a great relaxation position and is called the corpse pose because all the muscles relax. Your body temperature will drop, so you may need a light blanket.

Sankalpa affirmations

You may find the following *sankalpas* helpful:

Life: *From this moment on I am becoming stronger/healthier/healed/more confident/more positive about my life.*

Light: *I am more aware, more understanding, more perceptive* ... Or, *I am learning new skills and new attitudes.*

Love: *I am feeling more and more peaceful/happy/positive/relaxed/contented/balanced/accepting of my situation.* Or, *I am forgiving of myself and/or other people.*

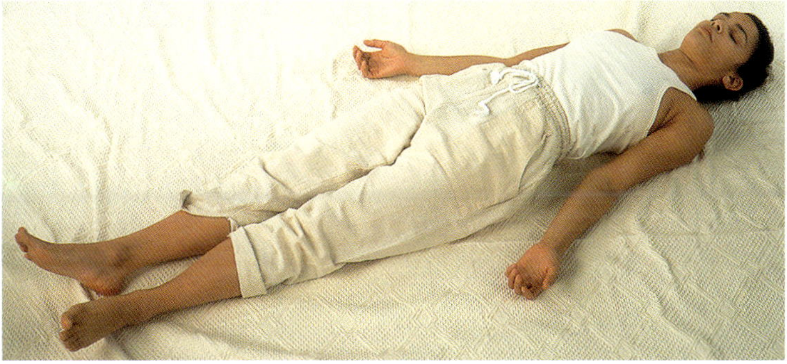

1 Roll the feet and hips in and out to find the best position, then roll the hands and shoulders in and out. If your chin juts up, place a small cushion under your head.

2 If your waist arches away from the ground, place a cushion under your knees. It takes time and awareness to find and settle into your most relaxed position.

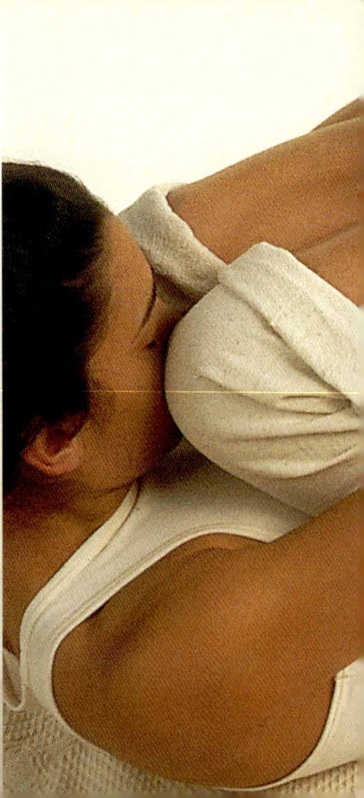

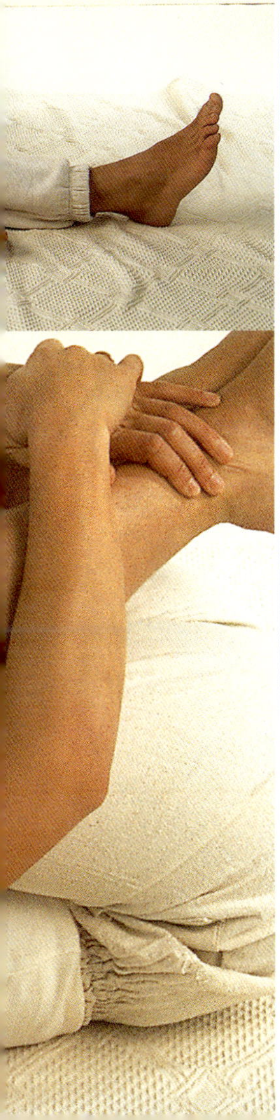

physical healing

Once you have understood the basic breathing, posture and energy principles of yoga healing – and have recognized the importance of self-discipline, self-awareness, and self-surrender as you practise yoga and live your life – you are ready to use postures for healing. Always start with warm-up stretches. Then move on to the specific postures to tone and strengthen the body, improve circulation, eliminate toxins and protect yourself against ill-health. With regular practise, you will gain stamina, greater freedom of movement in muscles and joints and increased vitality and wellbeing. Use deep yoga breathing to lessen the impact of daily stress and always finish your sessions with deep relaxation or meditation to promote healing at all levels.

How to practise yoga

We practise yoga techniques – posture, breathing, movements with breath and energy flow, classical poses, relaxation, resolve and meditation – in order to become "yogic" and to live daily life in the state or attitude of "yoga".

Yoga means union

Both yoga and true healing involve creating harmony between the five koshas – the physical, energetic, nervous, thinking and attitudinal levels of our being. The result is more abundant Life (energy), Light (awareness) and Love (receiving and giving).

What you need for practice

Choose a quiet warm space, with enough room to lie down and stretch. Wear loose clothing. Have a rug or shawl handy for relaxation and meditation. It is best to work on a non-slip mat or piece of carpet, roughly 180cm x 60cm (6ft x 2ft) and use a firm cushion or upright chair to sit on for breathing and meditation. Some extra small cushions are also useful.

▼ GATHER TOGETHER EQUIPMENT TO SUPPORT YOU IN YOUR POSTURES.

Set aside a regular time and place each day, to establish your "yoga habit". Practise yoga before eating, with an empty bladder and bowels. Wait about two hours after a large meal.

Which techniques to practise

Always involve all five koshas, however short your practice. Begin with a breathing exercise and careful spinal alignment to harmonize the nervous system. Continue with some stretches to release physical tension and get your energy flowing. End with relaxation and/or meditation to relax your mind and release negativity. Repeat your *sankalpa* (see Introduction) for healing, and to create beneficial changes in attitude.

▲ SIMPLE MOVEMENTS RELEASE TENSION AND ENCOURAGE ENERGY TO FLOW.

Several sequences are shown for you to "mix and match" to suit your energy levels. Choose to lie, sit or kneel if you feel weak or tired. When you feel energetic practise vigorously while standing, in order to develop strength and stamina. Rest briefly between sequences and for longer at the end. Practice should be regular rather than long: 15–30 minutes once or twice a day is ideal, plus a weekly yoga class if possible.

Every day is different and yoga brings improvements very quickly. Your own body is your best guide. Practise at what is a comfortable pace for you today, and for only as long as the exertion is enjoyable. If you feel breathless or shaky, take a rest and slow down your breathing. Resume your practice later when you feel better, perhaps choosing an easier sequence.

MAKE YOGA PART OF YOUR LIFE

Stay focused in your yogic attitude, whatever you are doing. Use odd moments for stretching, alignment, breathing or repeating your resolve – waiting for the kettle to boil, after long sitting or telephoning. There are many such moments in a day.

▼ YOGA CAN BE PRACTISED WHENEVER YOU HAVE A MOMENT TO SPARE.

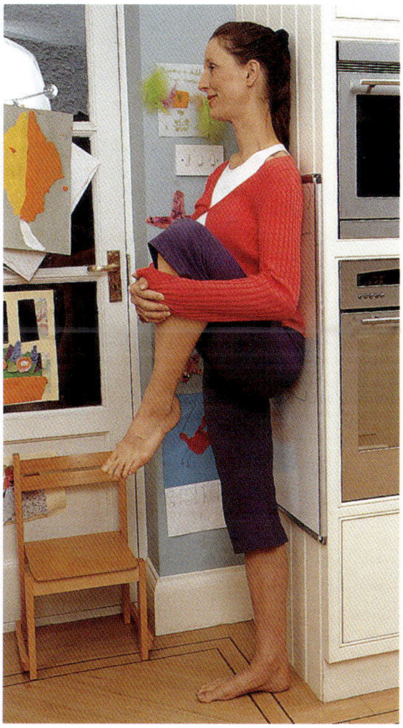

Getting started

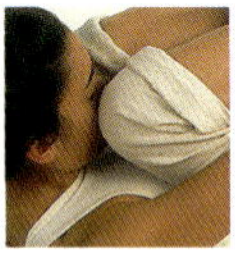

Start your yoga practice lying down if you feel stiff, tired or unwell. Allow gravity to help and support you as you breathe slowly and deeply and limber up gently to get your circulation and energy flowing. You will soon feel great.

Be gentle with yourself

Before you start, make sure that you are comfortable. Use pillows or cushions if you need support. If you are feeling unwell or are recovering from illness, take things very easy. If in doubt, consult your health practitioner before starting – but remember that yoga can work wonders at many levels, even if "exercise" is contra-indicated.

Breathing

Lie comfortably, with knees bent and head supported if necessary. Feel your energy moving as you breathe, travelling up through your body as you breathe IN, and down again as you breathe OUT. Let your breath soften and lengthen as you connect with the "tide of life" and float upon it for a few moments.

▼ *Savasana* is a traditional yoga pose – ideal for gentle exercise when unwell.

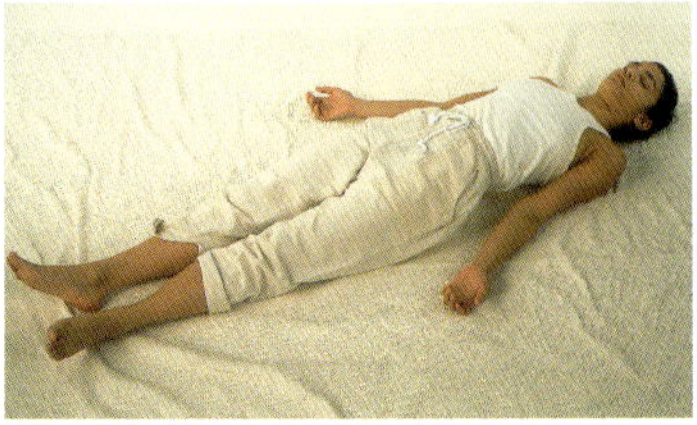

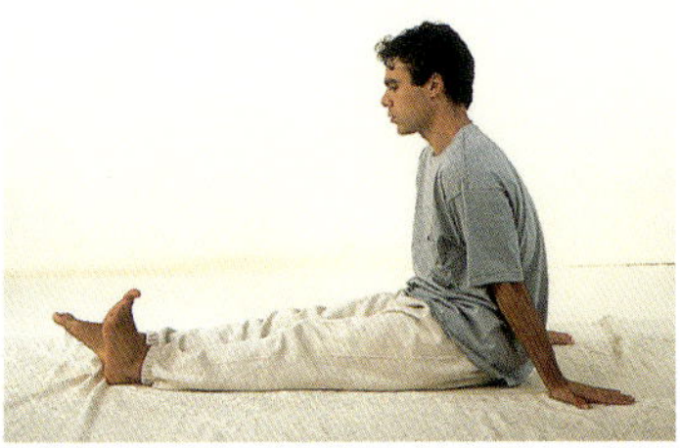

▲ Use yoga to dispel sluggishness and get your circulation moving.

Moving the extremities

Before you begin the postures, flex and stretch your fingers and toes, then your ankles and wrists. Move your feet and hands in circles in every yoga session and at odd moments during the day. Moving the extremities is the easiest and quickest technique to get the circulation and energy moving through the whole body. Practised regularly, this helps to remove congestion, stagnation, sluggishness and fluid retention, and wakes up the nervous system.

Pelvic lift

▲ Lie on your back with knees bent. Breathe IN to tighten pelvic floor and lower abdominal muscles. Breathe OUT to tilt pelvis and tuck tailbone under. Breathe IN to lift pelvis. Breathe OUT to lower. Repeat.

Knees to chest

▲ Lie on your back and clutch your knees to your chest. Hug with your arms and lift your head gently to your knees. Roll gently from side to side, then vigorously forward and back to sit up.

Lying twist

▲ Lie on your back with knees bent. Keep ankles, knees and inner thighs pressed together throughout. These muscles support the groin, pelvic floor and lower spine. Breathe OUT to lower the knees to the floor. Breathe IN to raise them (still pressed together). Repeat.

Seated forward bend

▲ Place your head over bent knees and gradually stretch out your legs. Keep your spine long and relaxed. Breathe deeply into the back of your chest a few times. Breathe IN to move energy up the spine and OUT to move it down. Unfold and return to *savasana* to relax.

Energy (Life) and balance (Light)

These sequences charge you with energy (Life) and wake up your mind (Light). Use them to start the day, or after too much mental work or enforced sitting. Always practise yoga in bare feet – unless stretching in public places!

DYNAMIC STANDING WARM-UP

Simply walking about on tiptoe is one of the best energizers there is. Standing on your toes strengthens your feet and ankles and relieves congestion, stagnation and fluid retention in the legs (Life). To stand on tiptoe and look up calls for balancing skills that sharpen the brain (Light). If your sight or hearing is impaired you will find balancing a challenge, so hold on to something, or practise with your back against a wall for support.

▾ STANDING ON TIPTOE STRENGTHENS MUSCLES AND SHARPENS THE MIND.

SQUATTING

To begin squatting, try leaning against a wall for support. Keep your heels a little way away from the wall to help you balance.

▴ Stand with your feet apart and hands on hips. Align the spine and tighten the muscles of the lower trunk. Breathe OUT as you bend your knees to the sides and lower into a squat, keeping your spine upright. Breathe IN as you rise to standing again. Avoid bending forward as you lower yourself down – hold on to the edge of a table if needed.

STANDING STRETCH

Stretching your arms overhead strengthens the chest muscles and opens the chest to allow better breathing. Keep your spine aligned and your arms well back, in line with your shoulders, to stretch the pectoral muscles and lift the sternum. Poor posture, fatigue and depression shorten these muscles and reduce the lung area. This worsens the poor breathing that created these problems in the first place. If, when you stretch your arms overhead, you feel breathless (through weakness or chest or heart problems), practise this exercise with your hands in *namaste* (prayer position) at heart level.

1 Stand tall, aligning your spine and distributing the weight evenly on both feet. Tighten the muscles of the lower trunk (Life) for strength to stretch up and open chest (Love).

2 Breathe IN, raising arms to sides and overhead, and coming on to your toes. Breathe OUT to lower arms and heels. Repeat vigorously until glowing with energy.

Positive feelings

These arm-circling, side-bending and twisting movements should all be done while keeping the lower body strong and unmoving and the spine in alignment. The movement is all from the waist upwards, in the thoracic area (Love).

Opening the chest from a strong base

These movements should be able to cheer up the gloomiest and most lethargic person, since they cleanse the lungs, improve the circulation and open the heart centre. Stand firmly with feet about hip-width apart, arches and inner knees lifted, back and inner thighs strong, pelvic floor drawn up, abdominal muscles holding the pelvis and spine in good alignment.

As you practise the movements, take your attention and your energy right into your fingertips. They are extensions of your loving heart, reaching out to embrace the world and everyone in it, including yourself. Feel that streamers of light are flowing out from your fingers in big circles up, down and around you, brightening up the atmosphere as you stretch and move through your whole body. For a less energetic version, the movements can also be done while kneeling or sitting cross-legged.

Arm circling

1 Stand with feet about hip-width apart and arms out to sides.

2 Breathe IN to raise arms forward and up. Breathe OUT to lower them back and down. Repeat several times, making big circles.

Chest opening

1 Stand tall with feet apart and arms in front at shoulder level. Keep your shoulders down and neck long throughout.

2 Breathe IN to take straight arms to sides at shoulder level. Breathe OUT to return them to the front. Repeat vigorously.

Side bending

▲ Stand with feet apart. Breathe IN, stretching your spine up. Breathe OUT to bend to the right, keeping the left shoulder back and in line. Repeat to left. Repeat both sides.

Rotating trunk

▲ Standing with feet apart, swing the arms and rotate the upper trunk from side to side, keeping the spine upright, the arms loose and breathing naturally and vigorously.

Breathing exercises

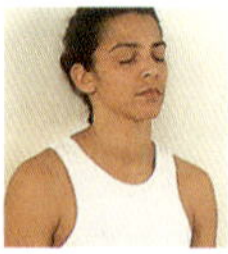

Yogic breathing removes stress. With practice, we can learn to de-stress ourselves in almost any situation, simply by breathing through the nose and engaging the diaphragm in slow, deep breathing movements for a few moments.

Shallow, stress-related breathing emphasizes the top and middle parts of the chest, similar to when we are panting from unexpected exertion such as running for a bus. Peaceful, rhythmical breathing engages the lower part of the chest and especially the diaphragm.

Yogic three–part breathing uses all the breathing muscles around the bottom, middle and top of the lungs. Stand, sit or lie and settle your breathing before you start. Just three deep yogic breaths may be enough to trigger the "all is well" response when we are feeling

THE YOGIC THREE–PART BREATH

1 Place your hands on your waist to feel the movement of the diaphragm and lower ribs as you breathe deeply IN and OUT.

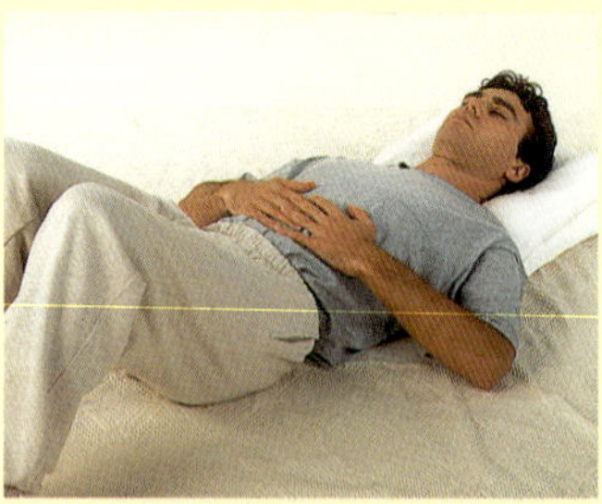

2 Now place your hands around the sides and front of the chest and feel the ribs opening and the sternum (breastbone) rising as you breathe IN. Breathe OUT and feel them retracting.

3 Then move your hands to your collarbones. As you breathe IN fully you may feel them move slightly.

4 Breathe IN from the base of the lungs to feel as though your chest cavity is filling with air up to the collarbones. Breathe OUT as fully and slowly as possible (residual air always remains in the lungs) to release tension.

stressed. This is the quickest and easiest way to control our nervous system and to calm it down when our mind and emotions have revved it up.

All yoga techniques exercise and relax mind and body. *Alternate nostril breathing* also restores the balance between them. Being too introverted makes us depressed or mentally exhausted and being too extroverted makes us physically exhausted. Mind and body are designed to work in harmony. People who spend too much time "in their heads" as well as those undergoing physical exhaustion, trauma or a life crisis, can benefit greatly from this simple exercise, followed by deep relaxation. You need to practise it on a day-to-day basis though, before turning to it in a crisis. Build up the number of rounds very gradually.

Alternate nostril breathing

1 Sit erect on a chair. Place index and middle finger of right hand on forehead with left hand in lap. Close right nostril with thumb and breathe IN through open left nostril. Close left nostril with ring finger and open right nostril. Breathe OUT through open right nostril.

2 Breathe IN through open right nostril. Close it with your thumb and open left nostril. Breathe OUT through left nostril. This is one round. Do several rounds then rest a moment with natural breathing, and observe how you feel. Repeat several times.

Balancing stretches

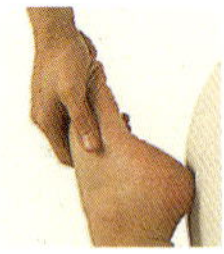

The focus here is on keeping the spine stretched and aligned all along its length while holding your balance – whether standing on one leg or both – and performing the different movements with deep concentration.

These stretches all require balance, focus and concentration, so they are good for Light energies (the mind). They also require a strong lower body (Life) and with regular practise, help you gain an open chest with relaxed arms, shoulders and neck (Love).

ISOMETRIC BALANCING

1 Stand with hands clasped and head bowed. Breathe IN to focus on tightening inner thigh and pelvic floor muscles. Breathe OUT as you raise arms to the sides a little and focus on squeezing "corset" muscles around the navel, pulling the navel back towards the spine.

2 Breathe IN as you rise on to your toes, raising your arms high to the sides and opening the chest by focusing on and squeezing the muscles along the upper spine. Breathe OUT to relax arms, feet, head and squeezed muscles. Do three rounds.

Chest and thigh stretch

▲ Stand on one leg and bend the other knee, holding the foot against your buttock with the bent elbow pointing back. Raise your other hand high in front, as though pressing it against a wall. It is helpful to practise this pose while standing about 15cm (6in) away from a wall, so that you have to stretch up and really open the chest.

Loosening rolling twist

▲ Rolling twists are energetic, so do them slowly and with awareness and stop if your breathing speeds up. Stand with feet about 75cm ($2\frac{1}{2}$ft) apart and hands on hips. Stretch up through the spine and push the pelvis forward with knees loose as you breathe IN. Breathe OUT to lean back from the upper trunk. Twist forward and clockwise in a fluid motion. Breathe naturally, focusing on maintaining strength and stillness in the lower body, with all the movement from the waist and upper spine. After a few rounds, repeat anticlockwise.

The tree pose

This sequence is excellent for spinal alignment and energy flow, as well as working the abdominal muscles. It works the legs strongly, opens the chest, raises the arms and engages the optical and balancing mechanisms in the brain.

Standing in the tree pose

Nearly all the classical *asanas* (yoga poses) work on all the energy centres along the spine, and the tree pose is a good example.

1 Stand with your feet hip-width apart and parallel, toes evenly spread. Feeling rooted to the floor, allow your right leg to float up, bent at the knee. Take hold of your right foot and position the sole firmly against the inner thigh of your strong, standing leg, with the bent knee out to the side, feeling the opening in the hip joint.

2 If you cannot achieve this position, place the sole wherever comfortable on the inside of the straight leg – what is important is to keep the knee back so as to open up the hip area. Realign your pelvis, tucking your tailbone under, and softly fix your gaze on a point in front of you to help you balance. When you feel steady, join your palms in *namaste*, breathing freely. Hold the position for several breaths, then breathe OUT to bring the leg and arms neatly down. Repeat the movement with the opposite leg.

3 Feel how the muscles on either side of your leg and trunk are working together, co-operating in the job of holding you upright and steady. Come out of the pose if you start to wobble. Once you feel rooted and secure in this pose, raise your arms slowly overhead, palms together, breathing in. Breathe deeply and hold the pose. Repeat on the other side.

Watchpoint

If balance is a problem, lean against a wall and experiment with the position of the bent leg until you find the best stance.

4 When you have worked equally on both sides, stand calmly to settle your body and breath. When you are ready, breathe IN to raise your arms over your head, being careful not to arch the lower back. Stretch right through from your heels to your fingertips and take a few breaths. Then breathe OUT to bend your knees as though you are sitting down. Keeping your spine as vertical as possible, lower yourself until you are almost squatting. Keep your heels on the floor. Take a few deep breaths in this position, then breathe IN to stand again. Repeat this “standing seat” several times.

Forward and backward bending

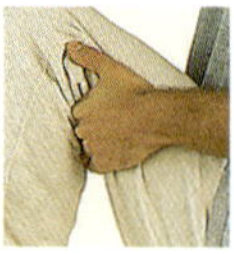

Many people bend forward by stretching their lumbar spine, with rigid hips and knees. This puts great strain on a very vulnerable area. Practising correct forward and backward bends gives you greater flexibility and a fully stretched back.

PREPARATION

This sequence is strong and dynamic. It requires some limbering movements first, especially in the upper spine, such as *opening the chest*. Movements such as *dynamic standing warm-ups* or *squatting*, strengthen the legs and feet and make the hips, knees and ankles more flexible. *Squatting* also trains the spine to remain upright when you are bending down.

▲ LIMBER UP FOR THE BENDS BY LIFTING YOUR KNEES TO STRENGTHEN LEGS AND HIPS.

PROTECTING THE LOWER BACK

Bending incorrectly – usually from the lumbar spine – is the most frequent cause of lower backache, especially when lifting. When you practise any kind of standing forward bend in your yoga sessions, first tighten your spine-supporting muscles and always bend forward with knees well bent and spine as straight as possible.

Your upper trunk and head are very heavy, especially if you let them sag like dead weights – so stretch the spine out and forward as you bend from the hips and take your body weight into your strong thighs. Your spine is precious and you can protect it by developing both awareness and lower body strength. Bend forward only as far as you can. Place your hands on your shins, ankles or the floor to support your upper body weight before attempting to straighten your knees. It is more important to stretch your spine than your legs.

Forward bending

Experiment with picking up a light but bulky box from a squatting position and then rise by straightening your legs – there should be no stretching in your lumbar spine (below and behind the waist) because your legs are strong enough to lift the weight of both your own body and the box. The muscles that hold your spine in place, which you have been strengthening through sessions of *body-mind breathing,* are protecting your lower back at all times. While in a forward bending position, with knees well bent and your head hanging down, you can release tension in your neck and shoulders by gently rotating your head.

Standing forward bend

1 Stand with feet about 75cm (2½ft) apart and knees well bent. Breathe OUT to bend forward and clasp your ankles or shins. Breathe IN. Breathe OUT to relax and let the spine lengthen, keeping legs bent.

2 On each breath OUT let gravity stretch your spine more, to get your best stretch for today. Finally straighten your legs if you can. Roll up very gently and stretch your arms up.

Backward bending

The aim is to increase flexibility in the thoracic spine (chest) without overarching the lumbar spine or the neck (cervical spine). Chest expansion exercises are a good way to do this. Practise this movement frequently as it's very good at relieving feelings of tightness and for improving breathing capacity. It is also a good way to warm up your spine before the back bends.

The neck carries all the nerves from the brain to the body. Congestion here is often caused by hunched shoulders, as we unconsciously attempt to "carry the world on our shoulders". Dropping the

Chest expansion

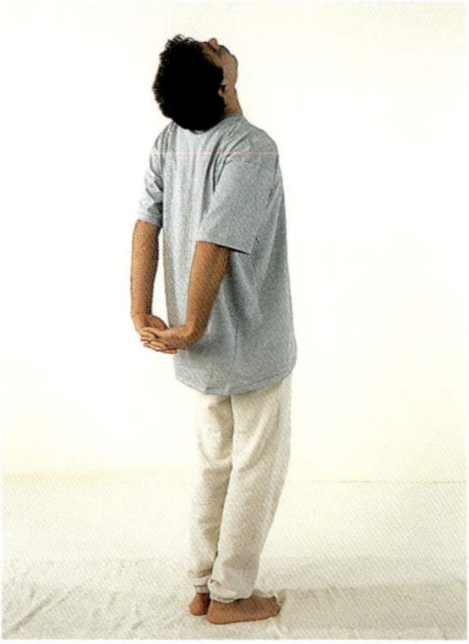

1 Stand tall and clasp your hands behind your back. Breathe OUT as you straighten your arms and lift them up behind you, keeping your lower body firm. Breathe IN to return your arms and stretch up through your spine.

2 Breathe OUT to bend the upper spine backwards, keeping your knees bent and lifting your straight arms up behind you. Take a few breaths in this position. Breathe IN to straighten up. Drop your head back only if it feels comfortable.

shoulders and opening the chest, as in back-bending poses, relieves this congestion, which is a common cause of headaches and feelings of acute tension. People who look and feel uptight are apt to have stiff shoulders, necks and thoracic spines because they are habitually "holding themselves together".

3 Breathe OUT to bend forwards with knees bent, lifting your straight arms up behind you. Take a few breaths in this position. Breathe IN to straighten up. Repeat this sequence frequently to open the chest and improve posture.

Watchpoint

The head is very heavy, so decide whether or not to drop it back. If your neck feels at all weak or uncomfortable, just look up and raise your chin as you bend backwards. As you come upright, lower your chin very slowly.

Standing back bend

1 Stand with hands on waist or lower back. Breathe IN and stand tall. Breathe OUT, pushing pelvis forward, bending knees and arching upper spine backwards. Remember to take a few breaths. Breathe IN to come up slowly.

Twisting the spine

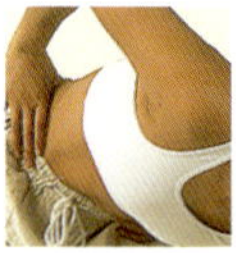

Spinal twists stimulate and strengthen the muscles on either side of the spine. These hold it in alignment by working equally on both sides. They also increase flexibility by contracting on one side and releasing on the other.

PREPARATION

Before twisting the spine extend it fully and avoid leaning forward or back. This allows the spine to twist from the waist upwards through the thoracic and cervical areas, opening the chest and stimulating the nerves that radiate outwards from the upper spine. A spine that is not fully stretched will twist too much in the lumbar area, rather than evenly along its whole length. This imbalance is a common cause of backache. Practise twisting movements after warming up well.

HELPING THE HEART AND CIRCULATION

All movement helps the heart and circulation (especially the diaphragm's movement when breathing slowly and deeply). Twisting movements also help to flush out the "used up" blood and toxic waste products that result

SIMPLE SEATED TWIST

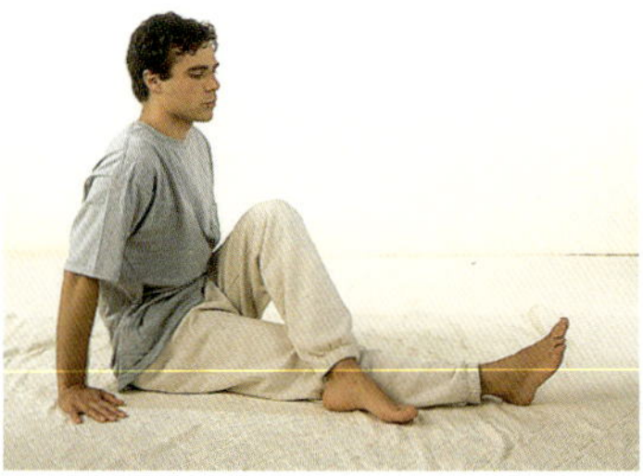

1 Sit tall, with your legs in front and your hands beside you. Place the sole of the left foot on the floor on the far side of the right leg. Breathe IN and stretch your spine up.

2 Breathe OUT to bring your right arm over the left knee and take hold of your right leg for leverage. Breathe IN to stretch up. Breathe OUT to twist. Repeat other side.

from energy production in the cells, and to get freshly oxygenated blood to every cell – especially in parts of the body that can be hard to reach in other ways.

Stretching the spine

First practise three rounds of *body-mind breathing* to tighten the muscles that support the spine. Keeping your mind on these muscles and the spine stretched up, breathe OUT and twist. This squeezes stale blood out of areas that can get congested – the abdominal organs, spinal muscles, lungs and neck. As you breathe in again and untwist, freshly oxygenated blood rushes into the areas that you have just squeezed.

Forward twisting

1 Stand with feet about 75cm (2½ft) apart and arms stretched out in front of you at shoulder height. Breathe IN. Breathe OUT and bring the right hand down your right leg and your left hand up above you in a straight line.

2 Turn your head (if comfortable) to look at your left hand. Breathe IN to straighten up into starting position. Breathe OUT to bring left hand to left leg. Repeat vigorously. For more twist, slide your hand down your opposite leg instead.

Kneeling sequence

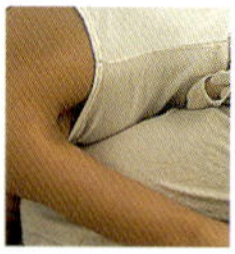

Kneeling or sitting is less tiring than standing, because gravity is with you rather than against you. These yoga poses work to loosen your upper back and shoulders, as well as your knees and ankles.

Preparation

Sit on your heels, with big toes turned in to touch each other. If your knees are stiff, place a cushion between your shins and your ankles. If your ankles are stiff, place a cushion beneath them until you are more flexible.

Child pose

▲ Sit on your heels and breathe IN. Breathe OUT to bend forward. Place your forehead on the floor, bringing your arms close to your feet. If your chest or bust feels compressed, you may prefer to rest your forehead on your fists or on a cushion. Breathe into your ribs at the back to expand your breathing for a few moments.

Flexibility in the lower body

Stiffness indicates poor circulation, usually due to lack of movement. Our skeletal and muscular systems are designed for movement – animals move from place to place and human "animals" have learnt to move on two legs, freeing the upper limbs. However, this puts great strain on the pelvis and lower back because they bear the body's whole weight. Yoga helps alleviate congestion, pressure and pain in the lower half of the body.

Strength in the upper body

The upper spine, shoulders and arms are also often out of balance because they do not carry enough weight to keep them strong. Again, yoga brings our awareness to this tendency. Bearing the body weight more equally in the all-fours position allows us to regain flexibility and relieve strain and congestion in the lower back, and develop greater strength in the muscles of the upper trunk.

Cat stretch

1 Sitting on your heels, stretch your hands forward along the floor, then raise your buttocks so that your shoulders are over your wrists and your hips are over your knees. Stretch out your fingers to make a broad base to take your weight. Breathe IN with your back flat and your neck relaxed.

2 Breathe OUT as you arch your upper back. Drop your head and look at your navel, tucking your tailbone under. Feel the stretch in the upper back. Repeat.

Back arch

▲ Sit on your heels with your big toes turned in and touching. Place your hands on the floor behind you with fingers pointing towards your buttocks. Spread your fingers and lean back with your wrists under your shoulders. Breathe IN, lifting the chest high. Breathe OUT to lower the chest. Repeat.

Watchpoint

When practising the *cat stretch*, ensure that your hips are directly over your knees. Keep the arms straight, with wrists directly below the shoulders and the fingers spread. It is the upper body that is being worked here, not the weight-bearing joints of the lower body, so focus on moving the upper spine, neck and head and keep your hips fixed.

Classical inspiration

Here we show an expert performing two modern classical poses taught in most yoga classes: swan stretch and dog stretch. This level of grace and flexibility is inspiring but all of us will benefit from our own practice of these positions.

INVERTED POSES

Wonderfully energizing, inverted poses are popular with yoga practitioners. The two best known poses – the headstand and the shoulderstand – are difficult to get into and dangerous to topple out of. A good alternative is the inverted *dog stretch*, where your head is held lower than your heart for a few minutes, but you are in a stable position. Begin with the swan stretch to elongate your spine and neck in preparation.

BENEFICIAL CHANGE IS HEALING

Even if we cannot yet achieve the perfect *dog stretch*, we can nevertheless work on those three basic activities that bring about the beneficial changes in us that we call "healing": self-discipline, self-awareness and self-surrender. More than two thousand years ago, the great yoga master, Patanjali, called them the "practical steps on the path of yoga". They underlie all healing and achievement – not only in yoga but also in other

SWAN STRETCH

▲ Sit on your heels with toes touching and spine straight. Bring your head to the floor (with your buttocks still touching your heels). Stretch your spine, taking your arms forward into the swan stretch.

aspects of our lives. Everything worthwhile requires enthusiastic practice, commitment and understanding of the principles involved. We need to let go of our negative conditioning, bad habits and poor self-image to move forward.

Watchpoint

If you have heart or breathing problems avoid the inverted *dog stretch*. Experiment first with a *standing forward bend.* You can either hold the forward bend briefly or come up to standing with each breath IN.

Dog stretch

1 Begin in the *swan stretch*. Shift your weight forward on to hands and knees in the *cat stretch*. Tuck your toes under. Lift your buttocks into the air, keeping your knees bent. Stand on your toes, taking your weight forward into shoulders, arms and hands. In this position, work to open your chest and bring your shoulders closer to the floor.

2 Finally, straighten your legs and bring your heels to the floor (if you can). Breathe deeply throughout, holding the position for as long as you can without strain. To come out of it, lower your knees to the floor and rest your heart in the *swan stretch* for a few moments before raising your head and trunk into an upright position, sitting on heels.

Final relaxation

Every yoga session should end with winding down, final relaxation and a "grounding" ritual. These practices may be the most important part of your yoga session, as they promote an attitude that brings deep healing at many levels.

WINDING DOWN

End your yoga session with some final stretching and some deep breathing. These are very relaxing activities, highly recommended at any time, and especially before going to sleep at night. They "switch on" the branch of the autonomic nervous system that activates the body's essential maintenance and repairs necessary for healing. Feel that "all is well" – as it nearly always is in the Now. This is a deeply peaceful and healing attitude in itself. We can always feel that way, even when stuck in a traffic jam. Why get fearful and uptight about something that is not a physical threat? Usually it is because we are reacting according to our outdated mental patterns of thinking.

These patterns, these basic attitudes, can soon be changed by practising our "all is well" yoga techniques at every opportunity, many times each day – especially when feeling stressed.

▼ *SAVASANA* IS AN IDEAL POSITION FOR MENTAL AND PHYSICAL RELAXATION.

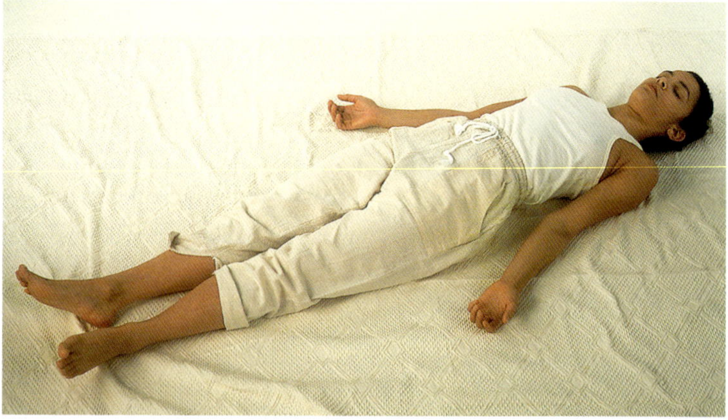

▲ If the small of your back arches away from the floor, support your head and bend your legs.

Final relaxation

This is "winding down" practised in a position (such as *savasana*) where the body is totally supported so that all muscles can relax completely. This, in turn, reinforces the attitude that "all is well" – otherwise the large "fighting and fleeing" muscle groups in the arms and legs would be clenched, and probably the jaw too.

As you relax, take your mind on a journey around your body to discover whether any muscles have tightened up again. If so, breathe OUT slowly while sending a message of letting go into those places that are holding on to tension. Final relaxation is not a time to fall asleep. Rather, keep an attentive mind in an inert body, watching out for the slightest tension in order to dissolve it.

Grounding

After 5–15 minutes' deep relaxation, come out very slowly, maintaining the inner attitude of peace and trust (Love), while being ready for and aware of (Light) the challenges of Life. Become conscious of your body and surroundings before sitting up. Once sitting, you can touch the ground with your head (Light) and hands (Love) as you celebrate your Life.

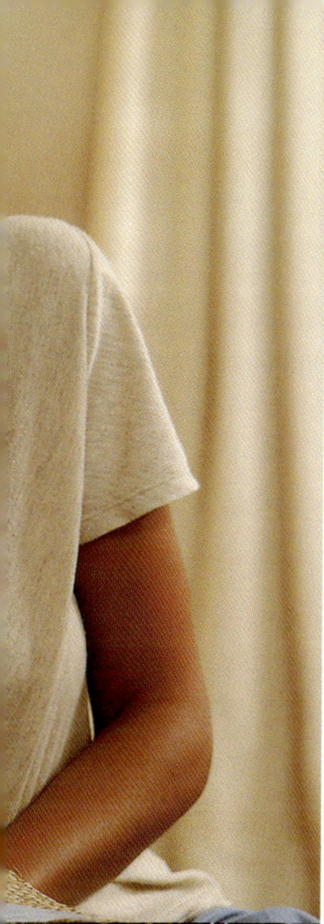

mental and emotional healing

The pace of life is fast and demanding and it is easy to get lost in the outer world. More and more people are suffering from stress-related illnesses ranging from everyday tension headaches to depression and serious nervous disorders. Many of these health problems can be related to imbalances in the chakras (energy centres). Yoga teaches us to "come back" to ourselves and helps us to explore our inner world using deep relaxation and meditation techniques. These have the power to refresh and renew us on a deep level, bringing healing from old wounds and a clarity of vision and purpose.

More about the chakras

The chakras correspond to points along the physical spine and seem to co-ordinate the emotional qualities and basic attitudes that create our "inner" world and reflect out into our lives. Balancing the chakras balances our lives.

We can change the state of our autonomic nervous system from the fright-fight-flight syndrome to "all is well" by working with the chakras. Use awareness, movement and stillness in those areas of the body that feel closed or weak and are in need of energy, healing and rebalancing.

▼ STRONG, EARTHBOUND POSTURES DRAW ENERGY TO THE LIFE CHAKRAS.

THE THREE LIFE CHAKRAS

These correspond to points on the spine in the abdominal cavity:

1 At the base (including the legs and feet). This chakra is concerned with physical safety/survival. Here we trust (positive) or fear (negative) the world. Yoga helps us to stand firm with strength and courage.

2 At the sacrum. This chakra is concerned with sexual/social interaction. Here we enjoy (positive) or shrink from (negative) the company of others. Yoga helps us to have more fun and friendship in our lives.

3 Behind the navel. This chakra is concerned with self-confidence. Here we work to succeed (positive) or are obsessed with self-image (negative). Yoga helps us to live our lives with enthusiasm and commitment.

THE TWO LOVE CHAKRAS

These correspond to points on the spine in the thoracic cavity:

4 Situated behind the heart (and including the arms and hands). This chakra is concerned with personal

▲ Straighten your spine and open your chest to balance the Love chakras.

relationships. Here we share with others (positive) or "keep ourselves to ourselves" (negative). Yoga helps us to accept both the joy and the vulnerability of relating.

5 Situated behind the throat (and including speech and hearing). This chakra is concerned with creative communication. We express our thoughts and feelings while listening to those of others (positive) or we choose to "hide behind words" without hearing (negative). Yoga helps us to share our truth more honestly.

The two Light chakras

These lie in the skull cavity:

6 Situated behind the brow. This chakra is concerned with mental activity. We focus our thoughts clearly (positive) or live in a mental fog (negative). Yoga helps us to relax and be more aware that "all is well" beneath the noise of our mental chatter.

7 Situated on the crown. This chakra is concerned with our attitudes and spiritual purpose. We grow in wisdom (positive) or stagnate in self-centredness (negative). Yoga helps us to relax and embrace ourselves and others.

▼ Practise forward bends to send blood to the Light chakras.

Relaxing body and mind

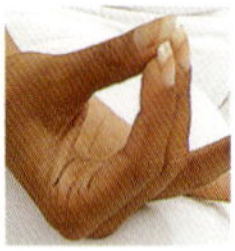

After relaxing body and mind we can unwind at those deeper levels where old fears, hurts and resentments lurk, sapping energy and joy. Once accessed, these "sore places" in our psyches can be healed.

Yoga relaxation

Follow the instructions, moving systematically "inwards" and then "outwards" again. With practice you will know what you can do in ten minutes or in twenty. Allow time to "return" to the everyday world and to ground yourself thoroughly. Practise daily and this technique will bring deep and healing changes. You could tape the instructions to play while you relax.

1 Remember your *sankalpa*.
2 Settle your body in *savasana* – you can cover yourself with a blanket if needed. Have your spine and head totally supported and your shoulders and hips loose. Once settled, do not move.
3 Settle your breathing.
4 Take your mind to each part of the body in turn and connect with that part. Always use the same order: right thumb, each finger in turn, palm, wrist, forearm, elbow, upper arm, shoulder, right side of chest, of waist, right hip, front of thigh, back of thigh, front of knee, back of knee, calf, shin, ankle, heel, ball of foot, top of foot, big toe, each toe in turn. Repeat on left side. Go around twice if you have time. This practice connects our minds with our bodies and heals the body-mind split that can cause many problems.
5 Move energy from the feet and up the spine – through the chakras – as you breathe IN and down as

▼ Placing blankets under your back helps to open up your chest.

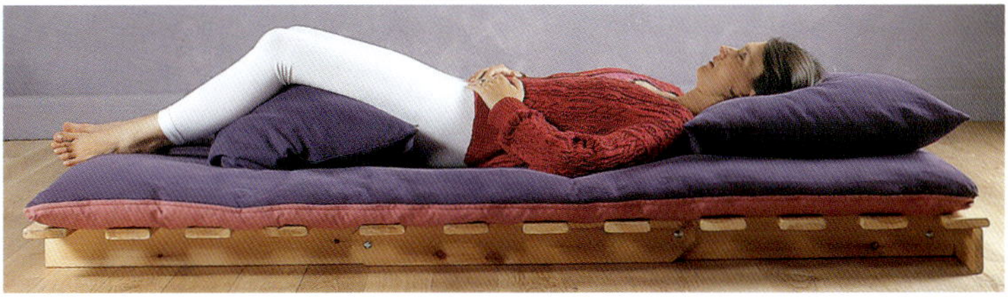

▲ You may find *savasana* easier if you support your knees and head.

you breathe OUT, healing and restoring balance at all levels. Wash away all burdens on the tide of energy moving back down to the Earth through your feet.

6 Visualize a place that means "spiritual home" to you – inside a sacred building, in a garden or by the sea, or in your own heart space where the Eternal Flame burns brightly. Settle yourself quietly and reverently in this space and feel its vibrations healing you.

7 Silently repeat your *sankalpa* three times, with deep commitment and intent.

Coming out of relaxation

When you are ready, start to come out of relaxation. Look at the place you are in and say goodbye to it, remembering that it is always there for you to return to. Begin to breathe consciously and deeply, revving up the "engines" of your body, ready for movement. Move your fingers and toes, your wrists and ankles. Stretch your limbs with a long, contented sigh, then a yawn, then a sigh again. Curl up, roll on to your side and sit up slowly when you are fully awake. Ground yourself thoroughly before getting up.

▼ Find your most comfortable position. Settle into it and relax.

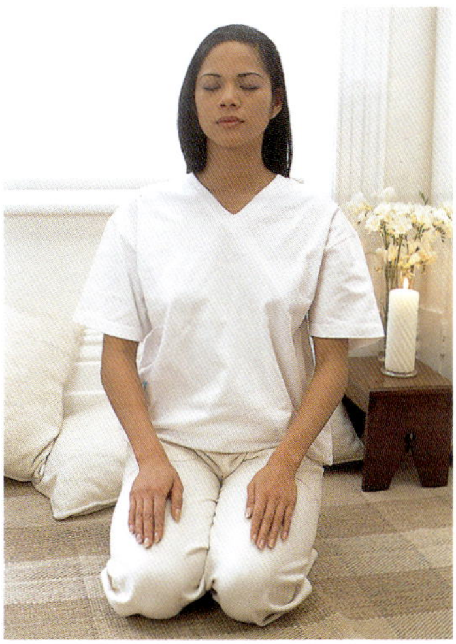

Stilling the mind

Meditation is done sitting up with the spine vertical. When the relaxation technique (previous page) has become second nature, use it sitting up, as a meditation, and notice the difference – your mind should feel very clear.

MEDITATION TECHNIQUES

To meditate, you need to settle your body into upright stillness. Look at the different positions on these pages and choose the one that feels right for you.

Settle your breathing. Breathe IN, taking energy up the spine, and OUT to take it down, until you feel quiet and relaxed. If you like, you can use a mantra with the breath.

▼ BEGINNERS MAY FIND IT EASIER TO SIT UP STRAIGHT ON AN UPRIGHT CHAIR.

▲ PRACTISE SITTING FREQUENTLY ON THE FLOOR IN THE LOTUS POSITION – OR CROSS-LEGGED IF THE LOTUS IS TOO HARD. CHANGE LEGS FROM TIME TO TIME.

A mantra is a sacred thought or prayer that is used in a number of eastern spiritual traditions, including yoga. *So haam* is a traditional mantra: in the Sanskrit language it means "I am" or "I exist". Think *so* as you breathe IN Life, travelling upwards through your chakras passing through Love on the way; as you breathe OUT

Light, think *haam* down through your chakras passing through Love again on the way down. This practice is very connecting. You are a child of Life and Light, created through Love. You also share your existence with others through Love.

When reconnected, you can focus on each chakra in turn, from the base up to the crown, quietly reflecting on the connectedness of its positive qualities and the isolation of its negative qualities.

▲ FOCUSED, AWARE AND STILL IN MIND AND BODY, IN A TIMELESS SPACE FILLED WITH ENDLESS LIFE, LIGHT AND LOVE. THIS "PEAK EXPERIENCE" IS THE STATE OF YOGA, WHICH HEALS YOUR WHOLE LIFE.

▲ IF *VAJRASANA* IS TAXING, PLACE A CUSHION BETWEEN YOUR HEELS AND BUTTOCKS.

Openness means love, and also vulnerability; being closed through fear means the loneliness of self-centredness. Healing is letting go of fear so that Life, Light and Love can flood our lives with joy.

After connecting with all your chakras and simply and easily accepting what you find there, close each one with a long breath OUT (from crown to base). Think of the chakras as windows that open into your inner world. Open their "shutters" to look inside yourself, but be sure to close each one before coming out of meditation to prepare you to re-enter the everyday "outer" world. Finish by grounding yourself.

Yoga and common health problems

Prolonged stress contributes to many health problems by overworking some systems and causing congestion or stagnation in others. Yoga rebalances the nervous system, removes toxic build-up from the body and is holistic.

Pollution in the body

The immune system is programmed to remove (through activities such as pain, inflammation, fever, etc.) all foreign bodies that enter the body. These can be bacteria, viruses, food additives, poisons in food, water and air, recreational and medicinal drugs (the side-effects). We ingest so much that is unnatural nowadays that the body gets stressed and confused as to what is friend and what is foe and starts attacking itself.

▾ A healthy diet plays an important part in boosting your immune system.

Many common conditions such as addiction, allergies, asthma, auto-immune diseases or chronic fatigue, are largely due to environmental stress.

The yogic answer to stress from pollution is two-fold. First, it works to reduce overall stress by rebalancing the autonomic nervous system so that the fright-fight-flight response is less easily triggered and the "all is well" response becomes the norm. Secondly, it tries to avoid ingesting pollutants through lifestyle and diet. This includes our diet of mental and emotional negativity as well as physical poisons. In the end, if we attend to the warning signals of distress, we create a happier and more fulfilling lifestyle.

Addiction

All yoga is very helpful. Relaxation with *sankalpa* and meditation brings release, healing and recovery when practised persistently with other (especially group) therapies.

Allergies

Regular yoga practice can reduce the need for medication. Consider your diet, as this is often how substances that are poisonous (to you) enter the system. Practise relaxation and meditation to reduce stress, as this can trigger allergic reactions.

Arthritis

Gentle exercise brings relief. If only some joints are affected, practise in the evening, having loosened up during the day. If inflammation is general the morning may be better. Avoid all exercise during a period of "flare up". Take great care with replacement joints and try to avoid positions that put pressure on weight-bearing joints. Choose sitting or lying positions for initial limbering and breathing and then do standing sequences slowly, with deep breathing and rests.

Asthma

Do what feels comfortable, slowly and without strain. Use your breath as a monitor, breathing deeply through your nose. Stop to rest at the first signs of breathing discomfort. Relax propped up. Watch your diet to avoid constipation. Relaxation and meditation reduce the levels of stress that can trigger asthma attacks.

▲ Do you have a favourite spot? Relax and spend time "just being".

Auto-immune diseases and chronic fatigue

Keep active and cheerful through regular yoga practice, but avoid stress and fatigue by relaxing mind and body and working with *sankalpa* for serenity and a positive attitude.

Back, neck and head pain

Pain and discomfort in these areas may be caused by poor posture, which can result from prolonged stress (feeling overwhelmed or defeated), lack of exercise and too much sitting.

Improving posture

Realigning the spine, gently and persistently through regular yoga practice, can change both posture and attitudes. Practise relaxation and chakra meditation (propped up to be upright and comfortable) to strengthen the positive aspects of the chakras – especially those in the region of the pain. Reduce stress by practising *alternate nostril breathing* and deep relaxation in any comfortable position. Work on the muscles that hold the spine in place with *body-mind breathing* and gentle isometric "muscle squeezing" to improve spinal posture and to reduce injury and the body's need to protect itself by going into spasm.

Lower back pain

Lie on the floor with knees bent to take all pressure off the spine. Move the spine gently to ease discomfort. The upturned beetle is also helpful: move the knees gently in all directions to ease the lower back. Move the head from side to side and loosen the shoulders for the upper back and neck. Keep the chin tucked in.

Headache

Pressure in the cervical or thoracic spine through habitually jutting the chin forward and/or slouching creates "traffic congestion" and is

▼ Back pain can be relieved by gently massaging your spine against the floor.

a common cause of headaches. Loosen the neck muscles with the head upside down in a forward bend, standing, sitting on a chair or lying prone over the edge of a bed. Take short yogic breaks between daily activities, especially those involving the eyes.

Cardiovascular/respiratory problems

These conditions result from long-term stress, when the autonomic nervous system's fright-fight-flight response is switched on more or less permanently, ready for "action" and "excitement". Eventually the overused systems falter, while the underused systems are unable

▼ To calm the mind, try this simple meditation. Look at a candle flame, then close your eyes, keeping the image in your "mind's eye" as long as you can.

▲ Inverted postures can help a headache, but be wary if you have cardiovascular or respiratory problems.

to provide essential nourishment, repair and recuperation. When the "all is well" response is blocked through prolonged stress we probably feel angry and exhausted. The yogic answer is to change our whole outlook upon life, to slow down yet keep as active as possible, and to learn to enjoy simple pleasures and a peaceful life.

Yoga exercise is helpful. Use your breath as a monitor, stopping if the breathing speeds up. Deep slow breathing, focusing on the OUT breath, induces a slow pulse rate and reduces stress. Avoid head-below-heart and arms-above-head positions if they make you feel breathless or dizzy. Relax and meditate regularly.

Depression

The term depression is often loosely used to describe anything from "feeling the blues" for a day or two to a prolonged and severe condition that requires medical treatment and supervision.

Yoga can alleviate this painful mental and emotional stress by rebalancing the Life, Light and Love energies. Focus on activating the Life chakras to increase vitality. Go for brisk walks and practise strong, invigorating standing postures to get the energy flowing. Depression can create deep fatigue, so exercise in short bursts with rests between each sequence – but do keep at it. Start and end your sessions with *alternate nostril breathing*. Avoid meditation and do not practise deep relaxation for longer than ten minutes, focusing on a positive *sankalpa*. Keep a spiritual diary to record and release distress. Re-read it periodically and notice how much yoga is lifting your spirits.

Digestive and other problems

The fright-fight-flight response, while revving up (and eventually exhausting) some systems, denies

▼ Be positive and value yourself – you are always your own best friend.

▲ Keeping a diary can help unburden you. Look back and see how far you have come.

energy to all non-essential functions at the same time. If this response becomes your habitual pattern, many of the body's systems (such as the digestive, eliminatory and hormonal systems) become depleted and will then malfunction or become diseased.

Yoga helps to rebalance the nervous system and reduce anxiety (and therefore the production of adrenalin). Avoid lying prone, or putting pressure on the abdomen in postures. Improve spinal alignment with deep breathing. Practise yoga before eating. Breathe deeply and relax often to reduce stress. Use *sankalpa* and meditate on the chakras and how both their positive and negative qualities promote or block the "all is well" response that creates healing and a balanced lifestyle.

▼ Standing postures can invigorate and lift your spirits.

Pregnancy

Although, of course, pregnancy is not a health problem, yoga can still bring many benefits. Recognize and allow for the tremendous changes to your body. Avoid carrying on with the same hectic schedule as before. Your baby needs space in your life, as well as in your body, in order to prepare for its birth.

Avoid all exercise for the first 14 weeks, practising only deep breathing and relaxation. From 15–29 weeks exercise energetically to open and strengthen the body. Avoid tightening the abdominal muscles or putting pressure on the abdomen. From week 30 onwards do not lie on your back. Relax supported by cushions, or sitting against a wall.

▲ Alternate nostril breathing is a balancing and healing practice and can be of great benefit when pregnant.

A few weeks after the birth start strengthening the pelvic and abdominal muscles with gentle exercise and breathing. Practise *alternate nostril breathing* and deep relaxation regularly.

▼ In late pregnancy, support your back, head and shoulders for true relaxation.

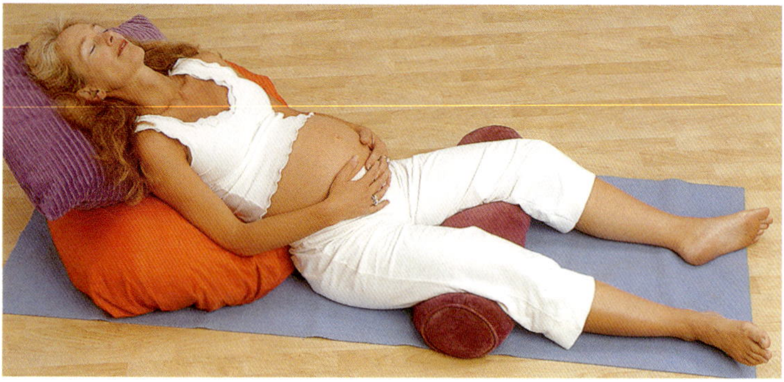

Useful addresses

For the worldwide holistic style of yoga taught in this book:

UK:
Satyananda Yoga Centre
A network of teaching centres, particularly in Europe, India and Australia. Tel: 020 8673 4869 for a list of teachers. They also sell relaxation tapes.
www.yogavision.net

USA:
Institute of Holistic Yoga
Satyananda Ashram
7970 SW 13 Terr.
Miami, Florida 33144
Tel: (305) 267 6772
www.satyananda.com
or
Yoga Journal
PO Box 469088
Escondido, CA 92046 9624
www.yogajournal.com

Australia:
www.yogavision.net, for addresses
or
Yoga Links magazine
PO Box 101, Campbelltown
SA5074, Australia
Tel: + 61 8 8369 0663
www.yogalinks.net

Other holistic yoga centres in the USA, Nassau and Canada:
Sivananda Ashram
Tel: (Nassau) 1 800 441 209
Tel: (US) 1 800 783-YOGA
Tel: (Canada) 1 800 263-YOGA
Email: Nassau@sivananda.org
www.sivananda.org

For yoga teachers recognized by yoga governing body in the UK:
British Wheel of Yoga
Central Office, 25 Jermyn Street
Sleaford, Lincs NG34 7RU
Tel: 01529 306851 for a list of teachers in your area.
www.bwy.org.uk

For yoga therapy by specially trained teachers in the UK:
Yoga Biomedical Trust
Yoga Therapy Centre
Homeopathic Hospital
60 Great Ormond Street
London WC1N 3HR
Tel: 020 7419 7195

For teachers specializing in prenatal and postnatal yoga:
Birthlight, 7 Essex Close
Cambridge CB4 2DW
Tel: 01223 362288
www.birthlight.com

Index